You Are Not Alone

A Book of Hope for Parents Dealing with Reactive Attachment Disorder (RAD)

By Kate Silvas

You Are Not Alone

ISBN: 978-1-4507-3901-6
Copyright © 2017 Kate Silvas

Bush Publishing & Associates books may be ordered at www.amazon.com.
For further information, please contact:
Bush Publishing & Associates
Tulsa, OKlahoma
www.bushpublishing.com

With all my heart,
I dedicate this book to the Glory of God, to Emilio
and to Cruz, Marelys and Miguel.
I love you all.

છ૪

The righteous cry out, and the LORD hears them;
he delivers them from all their troubles.
The LORD is close to the brokenhearted
and saves those who are crushed in spirit.

— Psalm 34:17–18

ACKNOWLEDGMENT

There are many people who helped me on the journey to this point.

Specifically, I would like to acknowledge and give thanks to Dr. Donald McCann, who has helped us and continues to help us through our healing process. I would also like to acknowledge the writings of Nancy Thomas (*When Love Is Not Enough*), whose work has helped me and many others on the path of recovery.

I extend my appreciation to Joanna Kaye, who has edited and helped me refine my manuscripts. My thanks go also to Lanny S. Lambert and Dr. Mary J. Riley for their review and encouragement. My sincere appreciation is owed to Pastor Donny West for my introduction to Margo Bush and Bush Publishing. I am deeply grateful.

I also wish to thank Jennifer Requena for sharing her talents and her professional photography. My gratitude also goes to Tami and Roland Benson for their expertise in marketing and logo design.

I would very much like to acknowledge the support of my mother-in-law, Julia Rodriguez, for her continued efforts in every way to help our family heal. I am grateful also for my sister Deine, who has listened and witnessed without judgment.

Most of all, my thanks go to my husband and very best friend, Emilio, for supporting me in my healing and in my writing.

Thank you.

FOREWORD

You Are Not Alone is a book of scriptural meditations intended for parents and primary caregivers of children with Reactive Attachment Disorder (RAD). While the message is intended for that specific audience, there are also those who are in difficult relationships to whom the message in this book will also speak.

RAD is a difficult psychological condition that children who have been in foster care or who have been adopted suffer from (and with) due to having been rejected, unwanted and, sometimes, abused. Significantly, we who care for these children also find ourselves victims of those rejections and injustices as we attempt to manage behaviors that can only be understood by those of us who live with RAD in our homes. We are accused of over-parenting our children, while we find ourselves afflicted with their rage and abuse.

Having failed to bond to a birth parent in the most important formative years (0–3) of their lives, RAD children have learned not to love, not to trust, not to feel remorse and not to allow themselves to be vulnerable. They hide or obfuscate the truth, steal, lie, hoard, manipulate, destroy property or possessions, kill or injure animals and sometimes kill or injure other children. RAD children act out in ways that defy explanation in an attempt to demonstrate—both to themselves and others—that they can control their circumstances.

RAD children think that because they were rejected in the past, they themselves are the only ones they can trust. Children who suffer with RAD refuse love from their primary caregiver, believing themselves to be somehow rotten and unworthy of love. Because of having been rejected, these children believe there must be something inherently wrong with *them* and, therefore, act out in the most insane, incredibly maddening ways to prove this belief to be true. The truth is, it is not true.

Unfortunately for us and our children, it is hard to understand that often their erroneous beliefs are a case of the sins of the past being visited on our children and on ourselves. Neither we nor our RAD children are to blame. That is not to say they cannot make better choices. They can. Nonetheless, the former, broken situation out of which they came to us continues to haunt them. And we and they are still feeling the ripple effects of those past events.

Enter the foster parent/adoptive parent/caregiver. Congratulations. Thinking that you and I can somehow give a nourishing, loving home to a child thoroughly convinced they are unworthy, we have exposed our hearts and lives in love to children who are completely afraid to love or to be loved. RAD children reject any attempt at normal love. Very few people can relate to this situation without having lived it. It goes beyond explanation, and so we avoid talking about the craziness. You may understand what I'm referring to: like all of the times you find food stashed under their beds or in drawers, because they are convinced you will not feed them. Or when you discover that something of significant sentimental value to you has been destroyed—just to make you mad. Or when you find that your child has once again stolen something from the store or destroyed something that belonged to someone you love. The list and severity of what happens goes on and on. I know all of these experiences, because I have lived them. I am one of you.

Once a child is diagnosed with RAD and treated through attachment therapy, however, there is hope. In the meantime, there is a long journey of healing, discernment, discipline and discovery.

From personal experience, I have found that few books really speak to the heart of a primary caregiver of a child with RAD, because it is an incredibly difficult experience. I have likened it to chewing broken glass. It hurts, and it doesn't seem to get better the more you do it. Often, the spouse cannot relate entirely, not being the victim of the inflicted abuse that comes with the territory. Other parents are confused by what they perceive as over-parenting on your part. They do not understand, because they don't live like prisoners in their own homes.

Normal parenting techniques do not work, so mainstream literature does not effectively address the needs of those in these unusual circumstances. It is extremely difficult to love a child who refuses and rejects advances of love time after time. It can break or even harden your heart, crush your spirit and rob you of hope. It can drive you to the brink of insanity. You may know what I am talking about.

There is good news, however. You are NOT alone.

This is the thing: God is near to the brokenhearted. The Bible addresses these conditions directly. It speaks to the brokenhearted throughout the centuries and tells stories of reconciliation, restoration and rebirth. No wonder it is called good news!

As a Christian mom of children with RAD and in any other difficulty, turning directly to God's Word for hope and reassurance—and answers—has helped me through those incredibly difficult times when the whole world seems to be coming unraveled. It literally is THE way up and THE way out.

If you are not a Christian, this book is also for you. It is my hope you will find wisdom in its pages that will speak to and heal your broken heart.

When you feel isolated, alone and abandoned, God is there. He is NOT silent. In fact, His Word is alive, and it speaks directly to your pain and suffering. He is talking to you. Yes, you, dear reader of this book, right now. The Scriptures are His personal love letter to *you*.

God has been there and has faced rejection and isolation. He knows your pain. He also knows the pain of your children. He has been there all along. My prayer is that the meditations that follow will help you draw closer to the One who was and who is and who is to come.

This book was written for you. God inspired me through His Word and gave me healing through these words to share with you. The words and meditations that follow are a path of healing for those who have ears to hear. I am simply putting them on paper.

Hang in there. You are not alone. There is hope. The Lord is near to the brokenhearted.

You are in my prayers as I write these words and even as you read them.

May God's peace be with you.

TABLE OF CONTENTS

༺◈༻

Your righteousness, God, reaches to the heavens,
you who have done great things.
Who is like you, God?
Though you have made me see
troubles, many and bitter,
you will restore my life again;
from the depths of the earth
you will again bring me up.
You will increase my honor
and comfort me once more.

— Psalm 71:19–21

CHAPTER ONE

WHAT IS THIS THAT YOU HAVE DONE?

Then the man and his wife heard the sound of the LORD God as he was walking in the garden in the cool of the day, and they hid from the LORD God among the trees of the garden. But the LORD God called to the man, "Where are you?"

He answered, "I heard you in the garden, and I was afraid because I was naked; so I hid."

And he said, "Who told you that you were naked? Have you eaten from the tree that I commanded you not to eat from?"

The man said, "The woman you put here with me—she gave me some fruit from the tree, and I ate it."

Then the LORD God said to the woman, "What is this that you have done?"

The woman said, "The serpent deceived me, and I ate."

— Genesis 3:8–13

As parents of RAD children, we are filled with questions. Unfortunately, we rarely get straight answers. We find ourselves facing sometimes very strange, inexplicable predicaments that are difficult to imagine or explain. Our child runs away. They lie incessantly—to the point where you must question everything.

1

Jewelry, medicine and things that matter to us just disappear. Expensive possessions belonging to relatives suddenly end up under our children's mattresses. Coke cans and candy wrappers are strategically hidden under couches. Smaller children are fair game as RAD children intentionally prey on and threaten them. Our children hide things—often, the truth—to make us mad, to control us, to make themselves feel powerful and in control. And there is so much more.

We ask our RAD children, ourselves, *God*, incredulously, *"What is this that you have done?"* It's as if we are saying to them, to ourselves, *"What were you thinking? Are you crazy?"* Our questions go unanswered. We are met with silence, anger and sometimes rage. There seems to be no answer.

Like us, God is in that very position in this passage from Genesis: *"What is this that you have done?"* (v. 13). Even today, God deals with children who have chosen to break the rules. Every parent faces that situation, RAD or no RAD. As RAD parents, the situations we face, are just . . . well, you know . . . heightened or surreal. Yet, here is God, in the beginning, interrogating His children after enjoying a brief period of unfettered relationship in the Garden of Eden. So if God knows everything, *why* is He asking *any* questions?

Answer: He is asking not to gather information but to see whether Adam or Eve—or *any* of us—will admit the truth. *"I hold the cards,"* God says to us, and with a broken heart, He asks: *"What is this that you have done?"* He knew what it would take to erase man's act of defiance—it would take sacrificing His Son.

Enter Satan. Adam blames God for placing the woman there; then he blames the woman; the woman blames the serpent. (I'm sure the serpent was smiling, thinking, "Aha! Gotcha!") God, in His wisdom, curses

Satan and disciplines Adam and Eve, banishing them from the Garden of Eden. Sin had just entered the very good creation that God had just made.

RAD or no RAD, we all face our sin, our frailties and the brokenness in the world around us. We ask the same question of our children, *"What is this that you have done?"* Sometimes there are just no answers, and sometimes the answers just don't make sense.

When we are children, choices are made that affect us—and the people around us—for the rest of our lives. I'll call the bad choices sin. Sin makes us question those we love and those who love us, as well as those who were *supposed* to love us: questions like, *"What is this that you have done?"* Unfortunately, as victims of our own sinful nature, we are prone to fail to see sin, particularly in ourselves. The Devil loves to pull the wool over our eyes.

By definition, sin is anything that separates us from God and from His will for us. God's will is this: for us to love and trust God and to love others as we love ourselves. But we all fall victim to wanting to put ourselves first. It's our choice. We either put ourselves on the throne of our hearts, or we place God there. It's that simple.

When we place ourselves on the throne of our hearts, that's called sin. It separates us from God, and it separates us from each other. We all do it, in one way or another, every day.

Yet RAD children are particularly prone to it. They operate from the premise that they are literally on their own. They just don't love or trust anyone. And they certainly don't put others first or feel any remorse about doing whatever they think is necessary to keep you from getting too close. It scares them to the point where they feel they must counterattack and do something—anything—to "control" or restore their environment. Here's why: because anyone they have trusted in the past has failed to come through for them. So they feel like, *"Why should I even try? It never worked before."*

Whatever they are, the sins of the past color us, our relationships and our view of the world. They also color what our RAD children think, how they feel—or don't feel—and how they think moving forward. Even with the most secure childhood, stuff happens. What is it like to be a RAD child? Think about it. *Why should they trust anyone?*

"What is this that you have done?" I would *really* like to ask that of the people who walked out on my children. It's hard. My RAD children are hurt, angry, afraid and *confused.* They won't say it, but it's true. I mean, the world has rules (you know, like the Golden Rule) that simply don't make sense to them. It does not translate in their experience. No one has treated them the way any of us want to be treated. So they think, *"Why does it matter? That's a stupid rule. I don't win that way."*

Here's the bottom line: it doesn't matter what happened so much as what happens next. Yes, your children have been hurt, and they have hurt you or hurt others. That's not the point. The point is, *What are you going to do about it?*

This is what God did: He laid down His life for us. That is the challenge. He loved like no one had ever loved before or since. He laid down His life for you, for me and for our children. Remember that. He loves all of us that much.

My heart was behind a brick wall for a long time (years!) from all of the anger, all of the disappointment, all of the stress and all of the fear. I had built the Berlin Wall between me and my children, practically complete with concertina wire, armed guards and everything. With help, prayer and determination, that wall is coming down, brick by brick.

There are days when the wall seems to reappear, just with a word or a glance. But the miracle comes when you *decide* and ask yourself, "*What am I going to do about it?*" And then, you just do it.

Turn to God, turn to the Bible, pray, exercise, believe. You Can Do This. You are awesome! Live it, because it's true. If it were not true, I doubt the creator of the universe would have laid down His life for you and me.

So when you are confronted with the question you ask of yourself, your children or whomever, "*What is this you have done?*" try not to dwell too long on the past. Accept the truth and move on. The real trick is getting to the place where you say, "*Okay, fine. This craziness happened. Whatever. What am I going to do about it now?*"

Make it count. Your children are counting on you. You are not alone. Hang in there. *You Can Do This.* [1]

---

[1]   This prayer has been attributed to the American theologian Reinhold Niebuhr; however, the real authorship is unknown.

ᬧᬧ

The Serenity Prayer

God,
Grant Me the Serenity
to Accept the Things I Cannot Change,
the Courage to Change the Things I Can,
and the Wisdom to Know the Difference.

— Amen.

CHAPTER TWO

WHY?

My God, my God, why have you forsaken me?

Why are you so far from saving me,

so far from my cries of anguish?

My God, I cry out by day, but you do not answer,

by night, but I find no rest.

—Psalm 22:1–2

One word, so powerful: *Why?* Do not pretend that word has not crossed your mind or your lips. We all want answers. We all want to know "*Why?*" As parents of RAD children, we often ask ourselves, our children and *God* that very question: "*Why?*"

Sometimes, we just do not know. Our spouse does not know. Our children do not know, or sometimes, at least, they pretend not to. Even if they do know, they may choose *not* to tell us in order to feel powerful. "*Why?*" you ask, time and again. "*Why, God?*" No one can tell us.

Sometimes, there is no explanation because there is simply and *absolutely no explanation*. Whatever it is, it *defies* explanation. Whatever the situation is, you may *never* know *why*. It's crazy because it *is* crazy. Whatever it is, it just does not make any sense. Whatsoever. The best thing to do is accept that it is just that way. Don't drive yourself crazy trying to figure it out.

God says this in Isaiah:

> *"For my thoughts are not your thoughts,*
> *neither are your ways my ways,"*
> *declares the LORD.*
> *"As the heavens are higher than the earth,*
> *so are my ways higher than your ways*
> *and my thoughts than your thoughts."*

— Isaiah 55:8–9

Thank *God*, because if that were not the case, you and I would have gone stark raving mad a long time ago! Why? Great question, but you may never really know. You must accept sometimes not knowing or being patient until the answer reveals itself. The best thing to do in the meantime is to take action. Require that whoever is responsible accept the responsibility for fixing whatever went wrong. Let *them* figure it out.

Go back to Psalm 22. Repeat the words out loud. Listen to them. Feel their power. Maybe you know them by heart or have heard them before. It is the Scripture that Christ began to recite on the cross.

> *About three in the afternoon Jesus cried out in a loud voice,*
> *"Eli, Eli, lama sabathani?" – (which means,*
> *"My God, my God, why have you forsaken me?").*

— Matthew 27:46

As a parent of a RAD child, you may feel alone; abandoned. No one seems to understand or can relate to what we deal with. We feel like our children walked in and God walked out. Not long ago, I saw a sign at a

YOU ARE NOT ALONE

church that asked, "Are you interested in being a foster parent?" I felt like scrawling the words, "Run for your lives!" on that sign. Maybe you understand.

In His suffering and abandonment, Christ was showing us what to do in that moment—cry out to God. Say to Him exactly what is on your heart. You don't have to use Scripture or a lot of flowery words. Just be honest—with Him and yourself. You may think God's not answering. The truth is, He has never stopped listening—or speaking or intervening—and He has *not* forsaken you. That is a lie that your enemy, the Devil, *wants* you to believe.

Instead, this is what God says to you:

> *"I took you from the ends of the earth,*
> *from its farthest corners I called you.*
> *I said, 'You are my servant,'*
> *I have chosen you and have not rejected you.*
> *So do not fear, for I am with you;*
> *do not be dismayed for I am your God.*
> *I will strengthen you and help you;*
> *I will uphold you with my righteous right hand."*
>
> — Isaiah 41:9–10

Hear His words. When you look at what He says about Himself, He uses all active verbs, statements of truth, of fact, about Himself, about what He has done, what *He* has accomplished.

Reread it again. This is what God says:

"*I* took you. . . ."

"*I* called you. . . ."

"*I* said . . ."

"*I* have chosen you. . . ."

"*(I)* have not rejected you. . . ."

"*I* am with you. . . ."

"*I* am your God. . . ." (*emphasis added*)

Notice how *passionate* He is. Think of Him speaking to you as a lover, as a friend, as your Lord, as your God, saying these things to you *personally*. Then hear the promises:

"I *will strengthen* you. . . ."

"(I *will*) *help* you. . . ."

"I *will uphold* you."

The God who created the universe, who is capable of great things, is making these promises to *you, today, right now, through His Word,* about what He *will* do for you! Think about it! <u>*God does not lie.*</u>

Little wonder, therefore, that He then gives us two very small instructions—of what *not* to do—in the midst of all these powerful statements about Himself and what He will do. He tells us:

"Do not fear," and

"Do not be dismayed."

He doesn't talk about what you have done in the past or what *to* do. He tells you what *not* to do: *do not fear and do not be dismayed.*

Why does He say that? Why is this relevant? He says it because He knows each of us personally. He knows the paths of our thoughts. He

YOU ARE NOT ALONE

knows what it is like to be fully human. Many of His children exhibit RAD behavior. He knows what you feel and what you are going through. He knows what it is like to feel totally cut off, isolated and abandoned. He knows because He has been there. He said it Himself. It is easy to miss it. Go back and reread the passages again and let His words sink in. Listen to Him.

In that dark place, when you are feeling abandoned, rejected, unloved and forgotten, God has *not* forgotten you. On the contrary, you are *always* on His mind. He loves you and your children very much.

> *"Can a mother forget the baby at her*
> *breast*
> *and have no compassion on the*
> *child she has borne?*
> *Though she may forget,*
> *I will not forget you!*
> *See, I have engraved you on the*
> *palms of my hands."*

Isaiah 49:15–16

God has not forsaken you. God is always with you, regardless of your circumstances. Turn to Him. The Lord is near to the brokenhearted. You Are Not Alone. Count on it. Always.

ᘒᘓᘔᘕ

Prayer of St. Frances De Sales
Do Not Fear
What may happen tomorrow.
The same loving Father
Who cares for you today
Will care for you tomorrow and every day.
Either He will shield you from suffering
Or He will give you unfailing strength to bear it.
Be at Peace, then,
And put aside all anxious thoughts
and imaginings.

CHAPTER THREE

WHAT DO YOU WANT?

The next day John was there again with two of his disciples. When he saw Jesus passing by, he said, "Look, the Lamb of God!"

When the two disciples heard him say this, they followed Jesus. Turning around, Jesus saw them following and asked, "What do you want?"

— John 1:35–38

Leave it to the creator of the universe to always ask the really important questions. Jesus gets to the heart of things. Sometimes, He asks questions that can make us feel really uncomfortable. What *is it* that you want? What *are* you looking for? Do you *know*? *What do you want*?

For each of us, the answer is very different, at different times and for different reasons. As a parent of children with RAD, I want them to be happy. Nothing more; nothing less. Just to be happy and healthy. To be children. To run, to laugh, to giggle, to learn, to grow up and to have a heart for others. That is my sincere desire. That is why I have children, why I chose to be a foster parent and why I chose to adopt them, to rescue them from a horrible life and to love them, to have fun with them, to teach them, to help them be prepared for life and to grow old and enjoy their company. To give them the second chance that I had when I was adopted. I want them to be honest, trustworthy and fun to be around. I want them to love others. I want to love and cherish them. I want them to realize just how fortunate they are.

However, what presents itself is often very different. The first day we met my son, he asked my husband a very courageous and honest question. "How long am I going to be here?" That was almost a decade ago. Though he is making progress, he is still asking that question in his words and in his actions. He wants to know, in his heart, how long before these people, too, reject me? He wants answers.

Children with RAD do not trust the adults, especially the moms, in charge of them. They have grown accustomed to trusting only themselves. They are surviving with the effects of what they have endured before we entered their lives. The adults in charge of them have hurt them, exposed them to untold horrors and rejected them. Thrown them away. Walked out. Forgotten them.

The problem is *not* these children. Sure, their behaviors are, well, just awful—unspeakable, even, in some cases. These children are *survivors*, cast off and alone. But what's left, the pieces they hold and the pieces we pick up of what's left behind, is just so very hard to handle, for anyone.

What is the problem? The problem is sin. Sin separates us from God and from each other. What happened to these children are the after effects of someone's sin and it is being revisited on them, on us and on our families. You can take charge and turn it around, but you will need help. Real, lasting change comes by submitting to authority greater than one's self. And there is no higher authority than God. He is in the eternal business of righting wrongs.

What do *our children* want? Answers. They want to know why they were rejected, hurt, wounded and abandoned. They want to know, "What could be wrong with *me*?" These children believe there *must* be something wrong with *them* that someone who *should* love them clearly did not, does not or failed to act as if they did. The reality is that there is literally NOTHING WRONG with your child. They just truly believe—and therefore act as if to prove—that they are bad children. They aren't. They are simply in a great deal of pain.

The result is that RAD children cannot and do not trust the caregivers that come afterward. Because the birth mom (or subsequent moms) failed to protect them from (or subjected them to) whatever happened, the mom to come often receives the brunt of the blame, anger and resentment. Believe me, I know.

What do these children want? Safety, security, someone to love them and tell them and show them that despite the prevailing circumstances, they are okay. They may not realize it yet, but they are not forsaken, forgotten or unloved. They are precious. They are important. Just like you.

Consider this: these are the very first words Jesus says in the book of John: "What do you want?" This is not an insignificant question. What *do* you want?

We all want a lot of things. And Jesus is asking a very important question. How do *you* answer that question? Be still and listen to the words: "What do you want?"

Maybe you know the answer to that question immediately. Maybe you have to think about it. Maybe the answer to that question is different today than it was yesterday or ten years ago and will be different tomorrow or even in the next hour. Jesus is inquisitive. He asked questions of His disciples and of the people around Him all the time. He genuinely wants to hear their reply, and ours.

The point isn't the answer to the question, whatever it might be. It is simply this: Jesus is asking. The One who created you and knows your inmost being is the One who is asking the question. He's not asking because He doesn't know. He wants to know if you know the real answer.

The reality is that He already knows the real answer. He knows what you want and what you need. He knows your circumstances. He knows you, your children and what they have been through and what they have put you through. He knows suffering. He knows the answers. He has always known the answers. Why do you think He is asking the question? He isn't looking for the answer. He's looking to see if you are ready to be honest with Him and with yourself. Can you say the words? Will you be honest with the answer? Will you still your heart and mind to know yourself what it is that you want? Do you know what it is?

Go back to the Scripture. Let's take it in context. What is going on? Jesus is being followed, pursued by two people who have just been informed by *their* teacher, John the Baptist, that Jesus is the Lamb of God. When they hear this, they follow Jesus. They don't think about it or say, "We'll get to it tomorrow." They just go. Jesus then turns around and asks them the question that is central to all our lives: *"What do you want?"*

Listen to the first two disciples' response to this question. This is their hearts' cry.

They said, "Rabbi" (which means "Teacher"), "where are you staying?"
"Come," he replied, "and you will see."
So they went and saw where he was staying, and they spent that day with him. It was about four in the afternoon.

— John 1:38–39

The first two disciples answered the question with the words, "Rabbi" and "Where are you staying?" The first word out of their mouths is true: "Rabbi." He is what they want. He is really what we all want, what we all need, whether we know it or admit it or believe it or not. "*Rabbi.*"

The next words out of their mouths are, "Where are you staying?" (It almost makes me laugh, really. The creator of the universe speaks to you, and you ask a question like, "Where are you staying?" It's almost as hilarious as the time when Jesus is transfigured on the mountain, and Peter in his nervousness makes the statement about building shacks for Jesus and Elijah and Moses.) I mean, really? "Where are you *staying*?" Is that what they want? What would *I* have said? What would *you* have said?

But Jesus doesn't laugh at them. I think He smiles, knowingly, and places the invitation at their feet, just as He does today: *"Come and you will see."*

Jesus answers them, patiently, simply, and as wonderfully as He does today. *"'Come,' he replied, 'and you will see'"* (v. 39). The Scriptures tell us they went and saw where He was staying and spent that day with Him. They responded to His invitation. They did what their hearts told them to do. They knew what it was that they wanted. *They wanted Him.* They followed after *Him* and spent time with *Him.* And really, that is all we truly want or need: Christ. A relationship with Him is what God wants from us, *for us.*

He created us to have a relationship with Him. He wants to spend time with us, and He wants us to spend time with Him. He created us, and He created the very desire in us to yearn after Him. He longs for us to turn to Him. He is the very thing that satisfies the desire He created in the first place.

He not only asks the question. He is both the Question and the Answer, the Beginning and the End. *He* is what we truly want, what we truly hunger and thirst for, whether we know it or admit it and whether we believe it or not.

"Come and you will see."

ᚘᚗ

The Lord's Prayer

"This, then, is how you should pray:
'Our Father in heaven,
hallowed be your name,
your kingdom come,
your will be done,
on earth as it is in heaven.
Give us today our daily bread.
And forgive us our debts,
as we have forgiven our
debtors.
And lead us not into temptation,
but deliver us from the evil one.'"

— Matthew 6:9–13

CHAPTER FOUR

I TELL YOU THE TRUTH

"For God so loved the world that he gave his one and only Son, that whoever believes in him shall not perish but have eternal life."

— John 3:16

I just absolutely love the book of John. In it we find so much about Jesus—so much wisdom, so much purpose, so much truth. John 3:16 is quoted often, but the passage is as rich and relevant today as it was the night He spoke these words to Nicodemus.

This is the message for you and for me today. Like us, Nicodemus comes to Jesus seeking answers, knowing—and confessing that he knows—that Jesus is from God. Jesus answers Nicodemus three times in the passage preceding this verse, repeating the words: "I tell you the truth." (See John 3:3, John 3:5 and John 3:11.) He is emphasizing these words, as if telling Nicodemus and all of us to *listen*. Repetition aids learning. It's like He is preparing us to hear it and receive it.

"I tell you the truth," Jesus says, over and over again. How many times have you wanted your RAD child to tell you the truth and yet the truth remains hidden? I have lost track. To say this experience is frustrating is an understatement. You want to pull your hair out.

Know this: your *real* enemy, the Devil, dwells in lies. Satan is the father of all lies. The Devil doesn't want us to know the Truth. Our enemy wants to convince us we are lost, abandoned, rejected, unwanted. Satan wants nothing more than for you and me to believe we are nothing to God. Uh-uh.

Jesus offers you the truth. This is the truth: you and I are special, chosen, loved and capable. When you make up your mind to, you *can* defeat the enemy's grasp on these children's lives and restore what the enemy has stolen, with God's help. Open your heart. Listen. Speak to Him.

"I tell you the truth," Jesus says.

God loves you.

ଔଈ

May these words of my mouth and this meditation of my heart
be pleasing in your sight,
LORD, my Rock and my
Redeemer.

— Psalm 19:14

CHAPTER FIVE

DO YOU WANT TO GET WELL?

Some time later, Jesus went up to Jerusalem for one of the Jewish festivals. Now there is in Jerusalem near the Sheep Gate a pool, which in Aramaic is called Bethesda and which is surrounded by five covered colonnades. Here a great number of disabled people used to lie—the blind, the lame, the paralyzed. One who was there had been an invalid for thirty-eight years. When Jesus saw him lying there and learned that he had been in this condition for a long time, he asked him, "Do you want to get well?"

— John 5:1–6

"**D**o you want to get well?**"** My initial response to this is of course he does! Why *wouldn't* he? But *does* he? He's been an invalid for *thirty-eight years*. Nearly four *decades*. It is really all he has become accustomed to. It is all he knows. Instead of saying yes, he says this:

"Sir," the invalid replied. "I have no one to help me into the pool when the water is stirred. While I am trying to get in, someone else goes down ahead of me."

— John 5:7

It is a long answer to a simple question. Sometimes we take a long time to answer a simple question. It sounds like yes, but it's full of reasons why he can't become well. In my family, we call them excuses.

But why did Jesus ask this question? It's almost as if Jesus asks the invalid this question in order to *prepare* him to be healed. In the same way, he speaks to us today. In our broken state, Jesus is like a careful, experienced physician. He knows where it hurts. He knows what to do. He asks you and me this question this day and every day, **"Do *you* want to get well?"**

I am faced with this question as I deal with my RAD children. *Do I want to get well? Can I help my RAD children get well? "Sir, I have no one to help me. . . ."*

Perhaps you understand. In dealing with RAD as a primary caregiver, you can find yourself suffering. I've heard it said that it's like helping a wounded dog. And it is. It's going to bite you if you attempt to touch it. There is no way around it. *How do you help someone heal when they are hurling all kinds of anger and rage at you?* You find yourself wounded and reactive. Our attachment therapist calls it Reactive Reactive Attachment Disorder. Many, many, *many* times, I have found myself—and *still* find myself—reacting in a negative way to my RAD children.

Perhaps you yourself know exactly what that is like. You offer love and get rejected. You take it personally. You find yourself with a broken heart, a broken spirit and a profoundly hardened heart. You find yourself shocked by the words that come out of your mouth or, worse yet, *how* the words come out. You ask yourself, *"Can I really be this terrible of a person?"* or *"How did this happen to me?"* You confront a person in the mirror who is not very nice. It can be devastating. You begin to question yourself and everything you believe to be true. It can tear your life, your family, your marriage—you—apart. It is difficult, no, *near impossible* to overcome. It sometimes seems like you are all alone and that no one, *not even you,* is or wants to be on your team. Believe me, I know. I've thought it myself. But I'm here to tell you that is simply not true. It is a lie that your enemy, the Devil, wants you to believe. Don't fall for it. *Do I want to get well? Yes! Yes I do! "Sir,"* you reply, *"I have no one to help me…"*

Then Jesus said to him, "Get up! Pick up your mat and walk." At once the man was cured; he picked up his mat and walked.

— John 5:8–9a

Here is the miracle: Jesus speaks and *at once* the man is cured. Notice how immediately that happens. He picks up his mat and walks. After thirty-eight years, he is healed. That is all. Jesus just opens His mouth and speaks. He does not hesitate. The invalid does not hesitate. Similarly, He speaks to *your* needs; *your* heart.

"Get up! Pick up your mat and walk." Jesus commands the invalid to *action.* Jesus is in control. He is in charge. Notice He doesn't say please. He commands the invalid to action. He speaks. He heals. He restores. And that is what He does and what He expects. He commands all of creation. And when He speaks, He expects us to get up, pick up our mat and walk.

Part of getting well—*being well—the act of being obedient and picking up your mat and walking—whatever that looks like—is believing* it can happen. Each time Jesus heals the blind, the lame, the sick and the dying He uses different means. Each time His method is different. The method isn't the point. The point is that He does it. But He requires the patient—you and me—to cooperate, to follow instructions, to listen, to do what He's telling us to do.

It may not manifest itself physically. I know that not everyone who is prayed for is physically healed. Children get cancer, our parents are diagnosed with Alzheimer's, and people close to us are paralyzed. Not everyone experiences healing in this life. It does happen, and in some cases it doesn't. I recognize that. However, that is not what I'm referring to. The physical is transitory. I'm speaking instead about being an invalid in the heart. That's where God dwells and longs to heal us the most.

This is a *spiritual* battle. You've been wounded. You're hurting. You're paralyzed. I get it. We—you and I—are not where we started out when we met our RAD children. It's changed us. We, too, are survivors. But the trials and the fires we go through as RAD parents and in life—they are what we endure to come out of the Refiner's fire as more than what we were.

Believing that it *is* happening, however, is what I'm speaking of. It can and it does happen. You and I just need to get out of the way. In our hearts and in our minds, we must get up, pick up our mats and *walk*! Seeing it happen and recognizing that it's happening... watching how it affects you and those around you is the fruit of the Spirit at work in you.

It may not be visible at first. It takes time. It may be gradual. It is fundamentally different for everyone. However, the God that parted the Red Sea *is* at work *today*. He is healing hearts and minds, each and every day. It may look nothing like it once looked or anything like you expect. Nonetheless, you simply must let the supernatural work unfold. And it *is* supernatural. You have little power over it, but you must cooperate.

"Get up, take up your mat and walk!" Jesus commands.

What does that look like? You will know. Pray. Remain calm. Exercise. *Believe.*

Your heart is broken, *tired*, and you may believe it is beyond repair. *God* can restore it. He *wants* to restore it. He wants to restore *you*. He wants *you* to experience *His* love, *His* healing and *His* peace. He *created* you. You *can* trust Him.

It is my belief that no manner of self-help books will *ever* solve the problems you and I or anyone face. Sure, they may provide a quick fix, but in reality, it is kind of like the blind leading the blind. We know nothing compared to God. You, by yourself, with the help of man, do not have the power to heal your broken heart, your hardened, crushed spirit. How can you and I possibly fix what we did not create? We can participate, but we do not by ourselves have the answer. Would it not then make sense to rely on the Word of God to solve the problem?

God is, after all, the creator of the universe, who knows all things, creates all things and is in all things, who loves you and your child with an eternal, sacrificial love.

Here are my two cents: if you do not have a copy of the Bible yet, get one. If you aren't reading it already, get busy. Then, get ready, pick up your mat and *walk*!

So how serious are you? *Do you want to get well?*

c3&

Psalm 23

The LORD is my shepherd, I lack nothing.
He makes me lie down in green pastures,
he leads me beside quiet waters,
he refreshes my soul.
He guides me along the right paths
for his name's sake.
Even though I walk
through the valley of the shadow of death,
I will fear no evil,
for you are with me;
your rod and your staff,
they comfort me.

You prepare a table before me
in the presence of my enemies.
You anoint my head with oil;
my cup overflows.
Surely your goodness and love will follow me
all the days of my life,
and I will dwell in the house of the
LORD
forever.

CHAPTER SIX

COME TO ME

"Come to me, all you who are weary and burdened, and I will give you rest. Take my yoke upon you and learn from me, for I am gentle and humble in heart, and you will find rest for your souls. For my yoke is easy and my burden is light."

— Matthew 11:28–30

I magine hearing these words from Christ spoken directly to you. His eyes meeting yours, His hand outstretched. *"Come to me,"* He beckons, *"and I will give you rest."*

Think of it: *actually having rest?* As RAD parents, you and I often find ourselves checking the boxes. Weary? Check. Burdened? Check, check.

We've heard it said that there's no rest for the weary. Uh-uh. *Wrong.*

But the wicked are like the tossing sea,
which cannot rest,
whose waves cast up mire and mud.
"There is no peace," says my God,
"for the wicked."

— Isaiah 57:20–21

Christ offers us—all of us—the rest we absolutely need. Notice who He includes: *"all you who are weary and burdened."* The whole world fits in that category. Why? Well, we only have to look around to figure that out. We were in the Garden of Eden. Then, oh yeah, that whole listening to Satan thing happened. We've been plagued with it ever since.

And notice how He says it: "I *will* give you rest." Not maybe, not hopefully, not perhaps. His Word is a promise. There's no backing down. He knows it, and we can believe it.

He's telling us the truth. He recognizes how hard it is, what we struggle with, what our RAD children struggle with. That's why He offers us the real thing. We need what He has to offer. *"Come to me,"* He entreats us. Why, then, would we turn to anything or anyone else? Stubbornness, maybe. Pride? Ignorance? Ego? He sees through it all. He's still offering what we need. If only we would listen to Him. . . .

"Take my yoke upon you and learn from me, for I am gentle and humble in heart, and you will find rest for your souls."

— Matthew 11:29

Okay, you and I want the rest, so what is it that He is telling us to do? *"Take my yoke upon you and learn from me. . . ."* The yoke He is offering us is similar to the yoke oxen wear. When pulling together, the two oxen are in step, side by side, accomplishing the work together. It's like Christ is saying, *"Trust me, I know how this works."* He even is specific in His instruction: *"learn from me."* How do I learn from You, Lord? Oh, I don't know, open the textbook, and do what it says! *(It's called the Bible! It's all in there!)*

Get this, okay? His yoke is easy and His burden is light. He tells you the truth. If it weren't easy or light, He wouldn't say that. How is it easy?

How is the burden light? Try this: if we would watch and listen to His instruction, His example, wouldn't life be a lot less burdensome?

We would see that we aren't the problem and our children aren't either. We are all created in God's image. That is not the problem. We are not bad. Our *behavior*—our desire to separate ourselves from God and take His place in our lives (sin)—that is what's plaguing us and our RAD children. Satan is at work in all of our hearts and in our minds and in our mouths, all of us. It's true. He's trying to win. It's up to us to decide: *Do we want to rest in the lap of the One who loves us and created us or . . . do we want to be tormented by our own selfishness?*

God is not going to check the box for us. He isn't forcing His way into our lives. He isn't like that. All He is doing is offering to be in our hearts and in our minds, next to us and with us, carrying us and giving us everything we need, including rest for our souls. That sounds like a pretty good deal to me.

So in the thick of the battle when you feel weary and burdened, turn to Him. Call on Him. Take His yoke upon you and learn from Him. What will happen?

"You will find rest for your souls"

— Matthew 11:29

ଓଞ୍ଚ

The steadfast love of the Lord never ceases; his mercies never come to an end, they are new every morning; great is your faithfulness.
"The Lord is my portion," says my soul, "therefore I will hope in him."

— Lamentations 3:22-24

CHAPTER SEVEN

JUST SAY THE WORD

When Jesus had entered Capernaum, a centurion came to him, asking for help. "Lord," he said, "my servant lies at home paralyzed, suffering terribly."

Jesus said to him, "Shall I come and heal him?"

The centurion replied, "Lord, I do not deserve to have you come under my roof. But just say the word, and my servant will be healed. For I myself am a man under authority, with soldiers under me. I tell this one, 'Go,' and he goes; and that one, 'Come,' and he comes. I say to my servant, 'Do this,' and he does it."

When Jesus heard this, he was amazed and said to those following him, "Truly I tell you, I have not found anyone in Israel with such great faith. . . ."

Then Jesus said to the centurion, "Go! Let it be done just as you believed it would." And his servant was healed at that moment.

— Matthew 8:5–10, 13

My daughter has RAD. One day, she said to me, "Mom, I want you to help me with my anger issues." That got my attention. Wow. I wanted to jump for joy! My daughter, who loves to subvert the truth, actually admitted something true and brave and asked *me* for *help. That* is a miracle. It is no small accomplishment for her and no small task for me, as I'm sure you are aware. It is a constant battle. I celebrate the small victories.

When you deal with RAD daily, it is a *huge* deal. RAD children are *convinced* that they themselves are the only ones they can trust. As a mom, you are *not* in the circle of trust. You simply aren't. It can be *very* discouraging. Shattered are the dreams of a strong, intimate bond with your child. It's gone. Sometimes it seems you are merely surviving from day to day. And the anger? Well, if you are not ready for it, it can pierce your soul. The daggers that can come out of their eyes when your RAD child decides you deserve it—well, I think you know exactly what I am talking about. Nothing can compare. You begin to ask yourself, what am I going to do? How am I going to build a relationship when my RAD child says with words or actions or even a look to go . . . well, you fill in the blank.

Here is the deal: you must *not* take it personally. It is NOT you. You must declare war on this condition and take over. Satan is the enemy. Your child, though they may act like it, is not the enemy. You are the adult, and it is up to you to begin to love with a supernatural love that will melt your heart—and theirs. You can do this. You must believe in the end result. Take action. Love does cast out all fear—yours and theirs. *Believe.* Believe that it can happen, that it will happen and that it is happening.

Once you do, incredible things begin to happen. When you believe in your heart that you can do this and act on that belief, your transformation is contagious. Everyone will notice. Your change from reactive to confident will challenge the system. You will begin to see things differently. Your heart will begin to heal. The child will begin to look at him or herself as you change. Your child will begin to realize that he or she is really only hurting himself or herself. When your RAD child gets angry—*and they will*—be sure that you challenge it and confront them with the truth: they are really only needing to accept responsibility for their actions and accept whatever consequences that make sense. For me, for instance, when I ask my daughter to do something and she refuses in anger, I get her to work out her anger physically. Push-ups work. Not too many, just enough to get her to stop and direct her anger to something physical instead. Each child is different. Chores are effective channels of energy and anger too. Don't back down. *You* are the one in charge.

Working through therapy and experiencing real healing is helping our family, and me, recover and heal. *Nothing is impossible for God. **Believe.*** God has entrusted you with a huge, seemingly insurmountable task, but He knows you. He chose you. He knows who is up for it. He is not in the business of making mistakes. He performs miracles. He's that good.

Did you notice what the centurion said to Jesus? *"Just say the word"* (v. 8). That's it. Four little words: "Just say the word." God has the power through His Word to create the heavens and the earth and all things visible and invisible, so why are we trying to accomplish in vain what He can do in one breath? We, like the centurion, are not worthy to have Him come under our roof. Yet, the centurion knows that Christ has the power to heal with just one *word*.

"Just say the word." If only we could be that centurion. Did you notice that Jesus was *amazed*? *Amazed*. Imagine that: amazing the creator of the universe! Isn't *that* astonishing?

You and I are amazing, incredibly brave parents. If you were not, I doubt that you would be reading these words. Be that centurion. Astonish God. Astonish yourself. *Astonish your children.*

Jesus speaks to those following Him about this man's faith, and He speaks to us this very minute. He underlines it with those reiterative words: "I tell you the truth." He wants us to sit up and take note: the omniscient God is witnessing to us that He has not found *anyone* in all of Israel whose faith compares to this man. Wow. I want to be that centurion.

Then He turns to the centurion: "Go!" He says, "It will be done, just as you believed it would." That's awesome. *It will be done.* Jesus does not lie. He is not like us. He will not and does not lie. You can count on it. He doesn't say, "It may be done," or "I'll think about it." No. He says, "It will be done just as you believed it would." God is giving you a chance. You have a choice. *Believe.*

"Go!" He says. "It will be done just as you believed it would." What are you waiting for?[2]

---

[2] *Episcopal Church. The Book Of Common Prayer and Administration of the Sacraments and Other Rites and Ceremonies of the Church: Together with the Psalter or Psalms of David According to the Use of the Episcopal Church. (New York :Seabury Press, 1979)* p. 833.

⳼

A Prayer Attributed to St. Francis of Assisi

Lord, make us instruments of Your peace.
Where there is hatred, let us sow love;
where there is discord, union;
where there is doubt, faith;
where there is despair, hope;
where there is darkness, light;
where there is sadness, joy.

Grant that we may not so much seek
to be consoled as to console;
to be understood as to understand;
to be loved as to love.
For it is in giving that we receive;
it is in pardoning that we are pardoned;
and it is in dying that we are born again to eternal life.
Amen.

CHAPTER EIGHT

FORGIVE . . .

"Therefore, as God's chosen people, holy and dearly loved, clothe yourselves with compassion, kindness, humility, gentleness and patience. Bear with each other and forgive one another if any of you has a grievance against someone. Forgive as the Lord forgave you. And over all these virtues put on love, which binds them all together in perfect unity."

— Colossians 3:12–14

This is a big one. Big. Huge.

Forgive.

"What? Who, *me*? I don't think so. I have every right to be angry, Lord! *You cannot be talking to me! Did you <u>hear</u> what he said to me? Did you even <u>see</u> that?* Are you *listening*? Were you even *there*? I cannot believe this. You *cannot* be serious! I'm entitled to my anger over

_____ ! (Fill in the blank.) *Do you even see what's happening here?"*

Yes. Go back and reread the passage.

Bear with each other and forgive whatever grievances you may have against one another (v. 13).

Forgive. Not just that. *Forgive as the Lord forgave you* (v. 13).

So you have a situation on your hands. You've been down this road before, a thousand times, and you know where it leads. You're tired of the same thing, the same script and the same outcome. It's almost like you've memorized the lines. No one's flinching: no one's giving in. You're fed up. What's next?

One simple word: *forgive.* Easy does it. *Forgive.*

Have you looked in the mirror lately? What do you see? Made any mistakes lately? Hurt anyone intentionally or by thinking only of yourself? Cut someone off in traffic? Performed character assassination or gossiped at the water cooler? Should I go on? Hmmm. Okay. . . .

Forgive.

This is the challenge. *Bear with each other and forgive. . . .* Why? *Because we ourselves are forgiven.* None of us is without sin, ladies and gentlemen. We all fail. We all screw up. We are all fragile humans. We are going to sin as surely as we breathe in and breathe out. Our thoughts betray us. We are mired in it.

But forgiveness, well, forgiveness is not something the Devil wants you to discover. But it is the way out. In short, it works. It is the key that will unlock the cell door to your enslavement to fear, rejection, anger, hatred, self-righteousness or self-pity and all other means by which we separate ourselves from our RAD children, from others and from God.

Try it. Do you know how freeing forgiveness is? If God can forgive us when we nailed His Son to a tree, well, you had better believe that it works.

It is not about the other person. It's about *you*. It's about you giving up and letting go. What's happened has happened. It's really up to you. It's you saying, "All right, that's enough, I'm not going to be a slave to this. I'm going to do whatever it takes. I'm going to forgive each and every one of the people who did these horrible things to me and to the people I love. I'm going to forgive *myself* for my inadequacies and poor choices. I'm going to forgive all of the people who have hurt me and my RAD child, either intentionally or unintentionally. I'm letting go of my anger and frustration with my child. I'm just going to let it go."

Then, watch what happens and what becomes possible. It's like suddenly you can breathe again. When you forgive—and I mean you *truly* forgive—regardless of whether it's sought after by the other person or not, you discover that the anger and resentment you held onto really was not hurting anyone else but *you*.

Let go of it. It's not helping you. Life is too short to spend it in self-pity and regret. Try it. You *will* be astonished. However, know this: no one can do this for you except *you*.

You were not created in the image of God by accident. You have the capacity to forgive as the Lord forgave you, because, well, you are His.

What do you want? Do you want to be well? Just say the word.

Forgive.[3]

---

[3]   *Discourse on Abba Philimon* from *The Philokaliai.*

ઉઠ૯ઝ

The Jesus Prayer

Lord Jesus Christ, Son of God, have mercy upon me.

CHAPTER NINE

I KNOW

This is what the LORD says: "... For I know the plans I have for you," declares the LORD, "plans to prosper you and not to harm you, plans to give you hope and a future. Then you will call on me and come and pray to me, and I will listen to you. You will seek me and find me when you seek me with all your heart. I will be found by you," declares the LORD, "and I will bring you back from captivity. I will gather you from all the nations and places where I have banished you," declares the LORD, "and will bring you back to the place from which I carried you into exile."

— Jeremiah 29: 10–14

Whenever I was sick or afraid as a little girl, my mother used to say these words to me: "I know." That's it. She would hold me, and she would place her hand on my back and move her hand in circles, repeating over and over two words of comfort and reassurance: "I know."

Like a loving mother holds her child, the Lord says the very same words to you and me in our suffering: "I know." Sometimes all we need is just to be comforted and reassured that there is, indeed, someone who does know.

Dealing with RAD in our homes makes us wonder: *Does anyone re-ally know?*

Yes, dear one, someone does. God knows.

Not only that, but He knows where you're coming from and where you are going. He knows what is next. And what is next after that. And what is next after that. He knows. We can hang our hat on His words and literally trust Him.

Why is it, then, that we would find ourselves doubting? It's easy when what we are confronted with day in and day out is extremely difficult behavior. God says it Himself:

"For I know the plans I have for you . . . plans to prosper you and not to harm you, plans to give you a hope and a future."

— Jeremiah 29:11

These words are not hollow or meaningless. He has plans for you. Not only that, but He has good plans. He intends to give you above and beyond what you need or can even fathom or imagine. He plans to *prosper* you and not to harm you. So why is it that we are suffering? Only God knows. I think it is part of the equation. It's like iron in a furnace. Exposed to the flames, we come out a lot stronger in the end.

Know this, however: God is on the other side of what you are going through. He is also in the middle of it, next to you, holding you, reassuring you, and telling you, over and over again, *"I know."* And He does know. He has been there and done that. He literally wore the cross on His shoulders, remember?

Did you see it? The Scripture says He declares it, almost like a battle cry. *"'For I know the plans I have for you,' declares the LORD"* (v. 11). It's really remarkable, actually. He declares it. It's not often that the Lord says He declares something. But here He is, saying it. He even prefaces the words by saying that He says it: *"This is what the LORD says"* (v. 10).

Did you notice what He says before He says the words *I know*? He says, *"I will come to you and fulfill my good promise to bring you back"* (v. 10).

It's literally that clear. In black and white. *"I will come to you and fulfill my good promise to bring you back."* He's promising this to His people who have been carried into exile. Believe me, I can relate to exile as a RAD parent. Sometimes it really feels that way. No one seems to understand.

Go back to the Scripture. It's as if the Lord is literally saying, "Look, I understand. This situation is less than ideal. In fact, it's pretty bad. I'm here for you. Don't worry. It's going to be okay. In fact, it's going to be a lot better than okay. You are not going to believe what I have in store for you. In fact, you are going to be amazed by it. Trust me. I've got this. You are not in control of this situation, so don't try to be. I am in control. Just understand that I'm bigger than this. And I'm going to rescue you from it. But you just need to hang in there a little longer. You're going to be okay. I've got you."

Just like the Lord, we have to stand in the gap for our children. Yes, the war is raging all around us and all around them. But it is not a war that we fight alone. It is a spiritual war of epic proportions, and we are in the midst of a barren place. Fear not. The creator of the universe is on our side. He will come to us. He says this to us just like He says to His people here: *"I . . . will bring you back from captivity"* (v. 14). It's a promise.

Know this: The Lord is near to the brokenhearted, those in exile, those mired in self-doubt and disbelief. He is near to me, and He is near to you. Go to Him. And you will find the comfort that only the Everlasting Father can offer. You are not alone.

"I know."

CʒʒჄ

☙❧

"You have searched me, LORD, and you know me.
You know when I sit and when I rise;
you perceive my thoughts from afar.
You discern my going out and my lying down;
you are familiar with all my ways.
Before a word is on my tongue
you, LORD, know it completely.

Search me, God, and know my heart;
test me and know my anxious thoughts.
See if there is any offensive way in me,
and lead me in the way everlasting.

—Psalm 139: 1–4, 23–24

CHAPTER TEN

BLESSED ARE YOU

*Now when Jesus saw the crowds, he went up on a mountain-
side and sat down. His disciples came to him, and he began
to teach them.*

He said:

"Blessed are the poor in spirit,

for theirs is the kingdom of heaven.

Blessed are those who mourn,

for they will be comforted.

Blessed are the meek,

for they will inherit the earth.

Blessed are those who hunger and thirst for righteousness,

for they will be filled.

Blessed are the merciful,

for they will be shown mercy.

Blessed are the pure in heart,

for they will see God.

Blessed are the peacemakers,

for they will be called children of God.

Blessed are those who are persecuted because of righteousness,

for theirs is the kingdom of heaven.

"Blessed are you when people insult you, persecute you and falsely say all kinds of evil against you because of me. Rejoice and be glad, because great is your reward in heaven, for in the same way they persecuted the prophets who were before you."

— Matthew 5:1–12

Blessed. Blessed. Blessed. While I know and acknowledge that Christ knows what He is talking about, the living of it seems awfully different in reality. *Blessed?* Please. I mean, yes, Lord, I know you're right, *but come on*. Blessed. I mean, hardly.

I don't feel blessed. How blessed do you feel when your RAD child hurls all sorts of anger and rage and defiance at you when you tell him or her to change her clothes to conform to the dress code? Or how blessed do you feel when the dentist expresses concern when they discover just how allergic your child is to following directions and brushing their teeth to the point that they grow orange plague to prove to you how in control they are? Blessed? Hardly.

Yet, we are—handling RAD for the umpteenth day. It hardly seems like a blessing when it appears to be the exact polar opposite, right? So why does Jesus say these words to us? What is His intent? What is the point? Why does it seem He is redundant in His message? Nine times over He says the words. *How can this be?*

This is what James the brother of Jesus tells us: "Consider it pure joy, my brothers and sisters, whenever you face trials of many kinds, because you know that the testing of your faith produces perseverance. Let perseverance finish its work so that you may be mature and complete, not lacking anything" (James 1:2–4).

Parenting a RAD child can be extremely defeating and rob you of the love you had in your heart. I think we can testify to the depth of the feeling of being poor in spirit. At one point, it's like we are spiritually bankrupt. There is nothing left. That is why Christ says this, I think. Hear Him again and reread the words and consider that we are blessed when we are the most humbled. We recognize blessing when we most need it. When we are on our knees begging for mercy, blessed are you and I, for our needs are the greatest, and we realize we cannot possibly do it on our own.

Then, here's the promise: ours is the kingdom of heaven. When we begin to realize in our deepest, darkest times how poor in spirit we are, how bereft we feel, it is at that pivotal moment God reveals Himself for who He is. He is our Father, our Provider, our King, our God. He longs to give us everything we need. Especially Himself. Blessed are the poor in spirit—you and I—for ours is the kingdom of heaven. What does that mean?

That means, I think, that in our sorrow, in our depravity, in our moment of greatest need, we can call on the mercy of the throne of God and all of heaven—legions of angels—will come to our aid. Yes. It's true.

"Blessed are those who mourn, for they will be comforted" (v. 4).

I don't really know what it is that you mourn for or for whom you mourn. While I haven't lost any lives to RAD, and I pray to God I never do, I have mourned other losses—my children, their pasts . . . hopes and dreams, my dignity and, yes, myself.

But there are those of us who deal with RAD who have lost the lives of children, animals and others to the effects of RAD. I cannot imagine the depth of the mourning of the parents of children who lost their lives in Columbine or any similar tragedy. But it is extremely disheartening and frightening to consider it and how prone our RAD children can be to harming themselves and others simply because they feel so alone and believe themselves to be bad children. I mourn for those children, the people they could have been, the happiness they could have had, the lives they could have led. It's nuts.

Yet Christ says we are blessed in our mourning. Our wailing for what is and what is not does not continue forever, does it? He doesn't answer that question. He simply says this: those who mourn will be comforted. And blessed are they. That means to me that God hears us in our crying, in our weeping, in our loss and in our hurting and will come to our aid to comfort us—in any form necessary that will reach us where we need to be met. It's a promise, really. It's not a maybe. He says you *will* be comforted. *Thank God!*

And that is the real challenge: gratitude. In the hour of our greatest need, are we then, at that moment, to turn our eyes heavenward and say, "Thank you"? I mean, really? Thank you? How thankful are we to have answered the call to foster or adopt children that don't want to be loved and reject us time and again? Yet these children are the ones whose hearts God is seeking to melt. It's so difficult in the middle of a crisis to consider it pure joy, is it not? Not long ago, I found myself asking the question, "Dear God, what could you possibly be preparing me for next?" Since then, however, I have stopped asking that question, because, quite frankly, I have found that I *literally* do not want to know!

Yet we are, in fact, blessed—*even in and despite our suffering*—in order to be a blessing to others, our children, each other. . . . "Consider it pure joy!" James exclaims (v. 2).

Take the challenge and be grateful. I have trained my children who refuse to be vulnerable to say thank you. They may not agree, but I ask them regularly what the four words are that never wear out: "Thank you very much." At least they will remember it after I am gone. Be a blessing.

Say thank you. It won't cost you a thing. But the reward? It is very, very great.

☙❦

"But to you who are listening I say: Love your enemies, do good to those who hate you, bless those who curse you, pray for those who mistreat you.... Do to others as you would have them do unto you.

If you love those who love you, what credit is that to you? Even sinners love those who love them. And if you do good to those who are good to you, what credit is that to you? Even sinners do that. And if you lend to those from whom you expect repayment, what credit is that to you? Even sinners lend to sinners, expecting to be repaid in full. But love your enemies, do good to them, and lend to them without expecting to get anything back. Then your reward will be great, and you will be children of the Most High, because he is kind to the ungrateful and wicked. Be merciful, just as your Father is merciful."

— Luke 6:27–28, 31–36

CHAPTER ELEVEN

BROTHER, LET ME . . .

"Why do you look at the speck of sawdust in your brother's eye and pay no attention to the plank in your own eye? How can you say to your brother, 'Brother, let me take the speck out of your eye,' when you yourself fail to see the plank in your own eye? You hypocrite, first take the plank out of your eye, and then you will see clearly to remove the speck from your brother's eye."

— Luke 6:41–42

This week, my RAD child pointed out to me during one of her tantrums that I always want everyone to be perfect. Never mind the fact that I had simply asked for teeth to be brushed and a shirt to be tucked in. Hmmm. Nonetheless, it made me wonder: do I, in fact, want or expect everyone to be perfect? *Is she onto something?*

I think that is what Jesus is pointing out to us in this passage from Luke. In our brokenness, do **any** of us get it right all the time? How about **any** of the time? **Who are we to judge anyone in any way?** Are any of us really all that perfect that we believe we are somehow entitled to throw rocks at each other? Of course not! "Brother, let me take the speck out of your eye," we say, ignoring the log in our own eye. *As if!* Never mind that we aren't God to begin with.

We aren't perfect, yet we are prone to judge and condemn other people, without mercy. *Why? What does it accomplish? It doesn't get us closer to God's will, does it?*

Can any of us really pretend to ourselves that standing in judgment of someone else helps us love them that much more? Isn't that Christ's central message: the whole love-thy-neighbor thing? Yet in our haste to label and judge others, are we not, in fact, pulling ourselves even further away from God's call to love Him and to love others? That, I think, is the point Christ is making to us. That is why He calls us hypocrites and why the whole world agrees with Him.

My children have heard me say repeatedly that what comes out of our mouths comes out of our hearts. (They have even repeated those words to others!) I believe those words to be true. Jesus says it Himself:

"A good man brings good things out of the good stored up in his heart, and an evil man brings evil things out of the evil stored up in his heart. For the mouth speaks what the heart is full of."

— Luke 6:45

Elsewhere in Scripture (Matthew 15), when the Pharisees confront Jesus about His disciples' forsaking the tradition of washing their hands before meals, Christ rebukes them:

Jesus replied, "And why do you break the command of God for the sake of tradition? . . . You hypocrites! Isaiah was right when he prophesied about you: "'These people honor me with their lips, but their hearts are far from me. They worship me in vain; their teachings are merely human rules.'" Jesus called the crowd to him and said, "Listen and understand. What goes into someone's mouth does not defile them, but what comes out of their mouth, that is what defiles them. . . .'"

"Don't you see that whatever enters the mouth goes into the stomach and then out of the body? But the things that come out of a person's mouth come from the heart, and these defile them. For out of the heart come evil thoughts—murder, adultery, sexual immorality, theft, false testimony, slander. These are what defile a person; but eating with unwashed hands does not defile them."

— Matthew 15:3-20

For this reason, I believe and tell my children that our words say more about **us** than those words ever say about the other person. When—*not if*—you and I judge others, are we not heaping condemnation upon ourselves? **Who do we think we are?** Are we not—you and I—saying to everyone listening that we have got these enormous planks jutting out of our eyes? Are we **really** that blind to our own sinfulness? What message does that send to anyone, especially our RAD children? Small wonder that Christ likens us to the blind leading the blind.

Jesus warns and instructs us, implores us even, through His words and by example. **No one is worthy to judge, except the Father alone.** Not even Jesus, as perfect as He is, serves as Judge. He says it Himself. By putting ourselves in that position of judging others, then, are we not putting ourselves in the place that God the Father alone serves? It's as if we somehow believe that pointing to someone else's sin is our job, when we forget all the while that we have this plank jutting out of our own eye.

Jesus calls us hypocrites, principally because, well, we are.

Jesus says this in part to shock us, to get our attention. Jesus can say it, principally because there is no plank in His eye.

In the first passage above, from Luke, Christ reminds us to pay attention and examine ourselves before admonishing one another. We—*I*—

59

often skip past that part, it seems. So eager to right someone else's wrongs, we just forget how we are all broken, fragile human beings, capable of greatness, yet continually wearing the Emperor's New Clothes as we parade around, judging others. It's like we seem to forget that we are all just ashes in the first place: "For dust you are and to dust you will return" (Genesis 3:19).

Why then, can we not all just have mercy upon, accept and love one another? Is it supposed to make us feel better to point away from ourselves as if someone else's flaws are greater than our own? Do we not all fall short of the glory of God?

As Christ hangs on the cross, the perfect sacrifice for our sins, Jesus begs the Father for forgiveness:

"Father, forgive them, for they do not know what they are doing."

— Luke 23:34

He's right. We didn't know what we were doing then, and we really, truly, even to this day have no idea. We're not just hurting one another. We're hurting ourselves.

Think. Your words and actions shout about you to everyone. Your children, especially your RAD children, are watching you. They are depending on you. Slow down. Be consistent. Pray. Breathe. These children are going to follow your example, regardless of what you may see or think or believe right now.

Those are some nice clothes you've got on, Emperor. Oh, wait. Hold on a minute. I have a whole sawmill in my eye.

୧ଓ୫୦

"Why do you complain, Jacob?
Why do you say, Israel,
"My way is hidden from the LORD;
my cause is disregarded by my God"?
Do you not know?
Have you not heard?
The LORD is the everlasting God,
the Creator of the ends of the earth.
He will not grow tired or weary,
and his understanding no one can fathom.
He gives strength to the weary
and increases the power of the weak.
Even youths grow tired and weary,
and young men stumble and fall;
but those who hope in the LORD
will renew their strength.
They will soar on wings like eagles;
they will run and not grow weary,
they will walk and not be faint.

— Isaiah 40:27–31

CHAPTER TWELVE

FINALLY

"Finally, be strong in the LORD and in his mighty power. Put on the full armor of God, so that you can take your stand against the devil's schemes. For our struggle is not against flesh and blood, but against the rulers, against the authorities, against the powers of this dark world and against the spiritual forces of evil in the heavenly realms. Therefore put on the full armor of God, so that when the day of evil comes, you may be able to stand your ground, and after you have done everything, to stand."

— Ephesians 6:10–13

He's sneaky, the Devil. He prowls around the dark recesses of your mind, lurking behind the slightest word, glance or thought, suggesting to you all the time how incredibly incompetent or unworthy or unlovable you are. Stop him right there. It is all a lie, a ruse.

He wants you to believe whatever he tells you. He likes to convince you that he doesn't even exist. Call him on it. He is an incredible liar. Do not listen to him. He's a born loser and he is not willing to let go. He wants to drag you down into his abyss of lies. Trust me on this. It's a trap.

The truth is that Christ is the Victor, and to Him go *all* the spoils. Truly, all of heaven and earth are under His feet. He is worthy and you know what? You are His. Which means, translated, that you are *right there with Him in the eyes of God*. His sacrifice covers everything, making you worthy in God's eyes. All is forgiven.

But beware. At the very moment you discover the Devil's schemes, you see him for what he is, you call him on it and you dare to show it to others—oh my goodness—watch out. He will turn on you. Count on it. Suddenly your entire life will be turned upside down in his efforts to pull you down and you begin to wonder why did all this chaos erupt? There's just no reason for it. Or is there?

I kid you not: the very day, no, really, the very *hour* this light turned on for me and I began telling others that it's really spiritual warfare in our midst—oh my goodness—at that very moment, all hell broke loose. My RAD child decided to pounce up and down on my other child's chest at the daycare—just because. And my husband was suddenly, physically stranded and in fear of losing his job. And I suddenly had a separate, unrelated car problem. I kid you not. All this happened at the nearly exact same time. Why? Do you really, really want to know? Do you really, really hear me on this? Satan loves to prey on us, and he will, especially when he feels threatened, when he feels exposed.

When you begin to see this condition—RAD—for what it is—the result of sin entering the lives of those who refused to care for your child—and that the Devil is behind it all . . . snap, crackle and pop! You can stand firmly on the Word of God. And your eyes will be opened. The suffering and the agony and the bouts of confusion and the frustration will not go away. But it will make life more tolerable, knowing it is a spiritual battle of epic proportions going on in your home and mine. Guess what?

God is on your side. And He will deliver you.

You and I are servants of the Most High God. He says it in His Word. True religion is this:

> *Religion that God our Father accepts as pure and faultless is this:*
> *to look after orphans and widows in their distress and to keep*
> *oneself from being polluted by the world.*

> — James 1:27

You've heard it, you've read it, and you *live* it, as do I. "*Look after orphans . . . in their distress.*" God knew when He breathed those words in Scripture what comes with the territory. He knew what we would face, you and I. It's not sugarplums and happily ever after. Everyone thinks it's idyllic, adopting a child. It isn't. It's messy. It's uncomfortable. It's *scary*, at times. You can't predict what will happen next. The other night, my son ran out the front door in his socks to get away from the consequence of once more hoarding a whole box of ice cream sandwiches under his bed. I mean, really? It's nuts.

It's kind of like being Alice in Wonderland—you're falling, you're falling, you're falling, down the rabbit hole. It's endless. You live like a prisoner in your home. I mean, who ever told you when you adopted that you'd have motion detectors, alarms on doors and video cameras to keep you and your family safe? I mean, honestly, I must have missed that part. . . .

The truth is you **cannot** parent a child with RAD without getting on your knees before the creator of heaven and earth and begging God for help. He's the only one we can turn to.

You and I are doers of the Word, and not hearers only. Make it your habit to immerse yourself in the Word, regularly, for your own sanity. It is your lifeline. The Devil is trying to get you to become unglued. Yes. That's the point of all this. He wants you. He wants your child. You absolutely, positively are smack dab in the middle of a spiritual battle.

Reread the passage from Ephesians:

"Finally, be strong in the LORD and in his mighty power. Put on the full armor of God, so that you can take your stand against the devil's schemes. For our struggle is not against flesh and blood, but against the rulers, against the authorities, against the powers of this dark world and against the spiritual forces of evil in the heavenly realms. Therefore put on the full armor of God, so that when the day of evil comes, you may be able to stand your ground, and after you have done everything, to stand."

— Ephesians 6:10–13

Put yourself in that passage, as often as you need to: minute by minute and hour by hour. Envision yourself cloaked in the armor of God. Write this Scripture down. Memorize it. Make it your mantra. Post it on your mirror. Recite it in the shower. Whatever it takes. Always, always, *always* remember that your struggle is not against your RAD child/children. It simply isn't. It is against those powers of the dark world that swirl around you, your children and your family, both visible and invisible.

Therefore, ladies and gentlemen, you simply **must** put on the full armor of God. It doesn't work any other way. Stay with me. Don't give up. Don't give in. Read your Bible. Do what it says. Hug your child, your spouse and yourself. You Can Do This. Hang In There. You **can** cross the finish line. Figure out what works best. Run. Walk. Exercise. Meditate. Do what you have to; try all of it or none of it. Just do something that will release that frustration.

But you absolutely must get on your knees and get in the Word. You've got to—for your sake and your child's. It is your only hope.

Amen.

EPILOGUE

In the months following my writing of this book, my eldest RAD child made a series of increasingly serious choices that forced us to conclude his needs could only be met in a therapeutic Residential Treatment Center (RTC). At present, my son is still waiting for placement.

It has been a difficult journey to get to where we are now. For many, many, many months, we looked and looked for residential treatment, only to find ourselves hitting brick wall after brick wall for a variety of reasons. There were few RTCs that offered the level of care my son needed, and those that did would only accept him at a certain age, or the waiting list was at least six months or the cost was about $500 a day. We found ourselves with fewer and fewer options while my son's condition grew worse and worse.

In retrospect, it appears as if each brick wall was not only an obstacle but also a message: God is in control, and we are not. Perhaps it was for the best, but we had to ultimately accept that, despite our best efforts, we really had no choice. As heartbreaking a choice as it was—and is—as his parents, we had to accept that joint conservatorship with the State was the very best and only real option to get him the help he needs.

We do know, without a doubt, we have done—and are absolutely doing—the very best we can. Even after five years of attachment therapy and eight plus years of treatment, we have had to accept that this young man whom we love may never be able to love or trust us in return. It's heartbreaking, but at the same time, we know we have literally done everything in our power.

I am still praying for a miracle.

I pray for you to discover God's presence along the journey and in the struggle. Miracles do happen. You are already that miracle to your children. This journey may not look or feel at all the way you and I expected at the beginning. And that's okay. It really, truly is.

Hang in there. You can do this.

I tell you the truth: You Are Not Alone. The Lord is near.

Made in the USA
Columbia, SC
22 October 2021